Pebble® Plus
Bilingüe/ Bilingual

Dientes sanos/Healthy Teeth

Uso del hilo dental / Flossing Teeth

por/by Mari Schuh

Traducción/Translation:
Dr. Martín Luis Guzmán Ferrer

Editor Consultor/Consulting Editor:
Dra. Gail Saunders-Smith

Consultor/Consultant:
Lori Gagliardi CDA, RDA, RDH, EdD

CAPSTONE PRESS
a capstone imprint

Pebble Plus is published by Capstone Press,
151 Good Counsel Drive, P.O. Box 669, Mankato, Minnesota 56002.
www.capstonepress.com

092009
005618CGS10

 Books published by Capstone Press are manufactured with paper
containing at least 10 percent post-consumer waste.

Library of Congress Cataloging-in-Publication Data
Schuh, Mari C., 1975–
    [Flossing teeth. Spanish & English]
    Uso del hilo dental = Flossing teeth / por Mari Schuh.
    p. cm. — (Pebble Plus bilingüe. Dientes sanos = Pebble Plus bilingual. Healthy teeth)
    Summary: "Simple text, photographs, and diagrams present information about flossing teeth properly —
in both English and Spanish" — Provided by publisher.
    Includes index.
    ISBN 978-1-4296-4600-0 (lib. bdg.)
    1. Teeth — Care and hygiene — Juvenile literature. I. Title. II. Title: Flossing teeth.
RK63.S3918 2010
617.6'01 — dc22   2009040925

Editorial Credits
Sarah L. Schuette, editor; Katy Kudela, bilingual editor; Adalin Torres-Zayas, Spanish copy editor;
    Veronica Bianchini, designer and illustrator; Eric Manske and Danielle Ceminsky, production specialists

Photo Credits
Capstone Press/Karon Dubke, all

The author dedicates this book to her friend, Liz Odom of Fairmont, Minnesota, whose path to self-care
began with flossing her teeth.

Note to Parents and Teachers

The Dientes sanos/Healthy Teeth set supports national science standards related to
personal health. This book describes and illustrates flossing teeth in both English and
Spanish. The images support early readers in understanding the text. The repetition of
words and phrases helps early readers learn new words. This book also introduces early
readers to subject-specific vocabulary words, which are defined in the Glossary section.
Early readers may need assistance to read some words and to use the Table of Contents,
Glossary, Internet Sites, and Index sections of the book.

Table of Contents

Tabla de contenidos

Why Floss?

Anna flosses her teeth once every day. Flossing cleans where her toothbrush can't reach.

¿Por qué hay que usar hilo dental?

Ana usa el hilo dental una vez al día. El hilo dental limpia donde no alcanza entrar el cepillo de dientes.

Flossing gets rid of food and plaque stuck in your teeth. Plaque causes cavities.

El hilo dental quita la comida y la placa que se te pega en los dientes. La placa causa las caries.

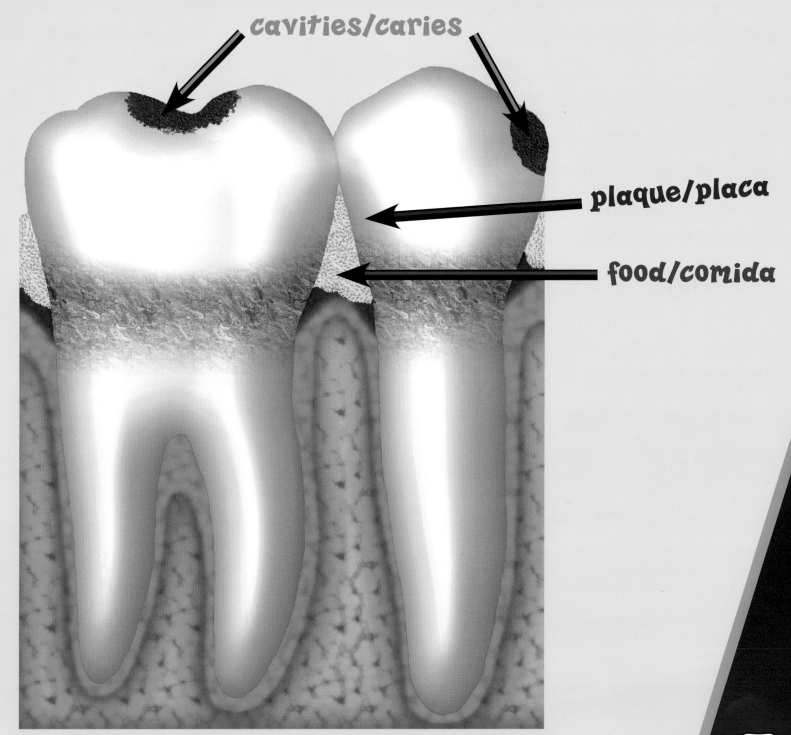

cavities/caries

plaque/placa

food/comida

Dental floss is a thin piece of string. Floss comes in many flavors and colors.

El hilo dental es un pedazo de hilo delgado. Hay hilo de diferentes sabores y colores.

Flossing

Anna pulls out a piece of floss about the length of her arm. She wraps it loosely around her fingers.

Cómo usarlo

Ana saca un pedazo de hilo dental como del largo de su brazo. Lo enrolla en sus dedos sin apretarlo.

Anna gently slides the minty floss between two teeth. She moves it up and down and back and forth.

Ana desliza suavemente el hilo entre sus dientes. Lo mueve de arriba a abajo y de lado a lado.

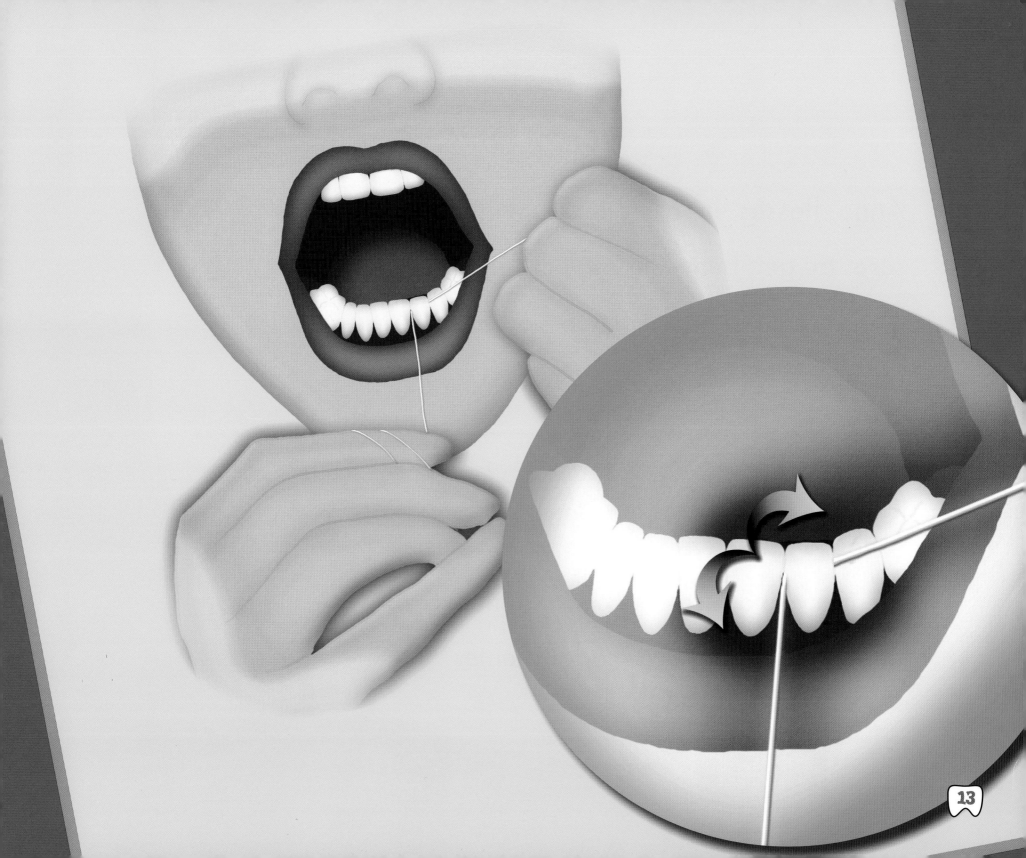

Anna flosses in a pattern. She makes sure to get between all her teeth. Anna uses a new section of floss for each tooth.

Ana usa el hilo con un orden. Se asegura de meterlo entre todos sus dientes. Ana usa un pedazo nuevo de hilo dental para cada diente.

Anna tries a flossing tool.
It makes flossing easier
for her.

Ana prueba una herramienta
para limpieza. Ésta hace más
fácil la limpieza.

Anna rinses her mouth after flossing. She throws away the used floss. She's done!

Después de usar el hilo dental, Ana se enjuaga la boca. Ella tira el hilo dental usado. ¡Ya terminó!

Healthy Teeth

Flossing your teeth will help you have a healthy smile too!

Dientes Sanos

¡El uso del hilo dental también te sirve para tener una sonrisa sana!

Glossary

cavity — a decayed part or hole in a tooth

gum — the firm skin around the base of a tooth

length — the distance from one end of something to the other

pattern — a repeated set of actions; flossing in the same pattern helps you remember to get between all of your teeth every time you floss.

plaque — a sticky coating that forms on your teeth from food, bacteria, and saliva in your mouth

tooth — one of the white, bony parts of your mouth that you use for biting and chewing food

Internet Sites

FactHound offers a safe, fun way to find Internet sites related to this book. All of the sites on FactHound have been researched by our staff.

Here's all you do:

Visit *www.facthound.com*

FactHound will fetch the best sites for you!

Glosario

la carie — parte carcomida o agujero en el diente

el diente — una de las partes blancas y huesudas de tu boca que usas para morder y masticar la comida

la encía — la piel firme que rodea la base del diente

el largo — distancia de un punto a otro

el orden — repetir un conjunto de acciones; el uso del hilo dental con un mismo orden te ayuda a recordar a meterlo entre todos tus dientes cada vez que los limpias.

la placa — una capa pegajosa que se forma en tus dientes por la comida, gérmenes y saliva en tu boca

Sitios de Internet

FactHound brinda una forma segura y divertida de encontrar sitios de Internet relacionados con este libro. Todos los sitios en FactHound han sido investigados por nuestro personal.

Esto es todo lo que tú necesitas hacer:

Visita *www.facthound.com*

¡FactHound buscará los mejores sitios para ti!

Index

índice